Who Was Saint Patrick

By Christopher Forest

2015
Outback Books

Shamrocks are green
Glasses help you look
Thanks so much
For reading this book

Outback Books

Meet St. Patrick

We acknowledge that all facts are believed to be true
at the time of this printing.

Summary: A brief look at the life of St. Patrick
from his early years to his sainthood.

Author: Christopher Forest
Editor: Melissa Forest
ISBN: 978-1508721949

Outbook Books
A division of Outhouse Books
Danvers, MA 01923
1 2 3 4 5 6 7 8 9 0 1

St. Patrick's Day is a favorite holiday. It is a day when we think about St. Patrick. He was a man who once lived in the country of Ireland.

St. Patrick lived more than 1500 years ago. He was born in a country known as England. His mother and father owned a lot of land.

When he was sixteen, men kidnapped St. Patrick. They took him to Ireland and made him a slave. He lived in Ireland for six years. He worked as a shepherd.

While in Ireland, St. Patrick spent many days by himself. One day, he heard a voice calling to him. He believed it was God. God told him to leave Ireland and return home. St. Patrick escaped.

When he returned home, St. Patrick decided to become a priest. Priests are people who teach about God. He went to school and studied hard. Patrick became a priest. He decided to move back to Ireland to teach about God.

In Ireland, Patrick spoke about God. He combined the beliefs of God with older beliefs. He used a shamrock to teach that God had three forms. Many people listened to Patrick. They began to believe in his God.

People trusted St. Patrick. Many stories were told about him. Some people even claimed he chased all of the snakes out of Ireland. This is probably not true. But, Patrick was considered a great man.

St. Patrick probably died on March 17 in the year 460. Soon after, people began to remember all the good deeds he did.

People made March 17th the official day to honor him. That is why March 17th is St. Patrick's Day.

Today we remember St. Patrick on this day. It is also a day to think about Ireland. So, on March 17th, we celebrate many Irish customs.

HAPPY
ST. PATRICK'S
DAY
TO YOU

♣

Picture credits

62514698R00015